From Fantasy to Reality: Real Talk on Early Motherhood from a Therapist Mom

A Creative Resource for Pregnancy, Postpartum, Parenting, and Everything in Between

by Yuliya Golubev

Art & Creative Prompts by Sharon Itkoff Nacache

From Fantasy to Reality: Real Talk on Early Motherhood from a Therapist Mom

Book Testimonials

"Drawing on extensive experience and a profound understanding of maternal mental health, Yuliya has created a thoughtful, witty, and compassionate guide for navigating the challenges of early motherhood. This book offers both practical guidance and emotional support, helping mothers feel seen, supported, and empowered throughout the postpartum period."

-Astrid Haroian

Psychoanalyst and Gestalt Psychotherapist in Training
First-time Mother

"As a fellow Gestalt psychotherapist and mother, I appreciated the way Yuliya Golubev weaves together professional wisdom with the lived experience of parenting, creating a resource that is both practical and profoundly human. The reflective prompts and creative art-based practices by Sharon Itkoff Nacashe make this book especially approachable for new mothers in a format that is easy to engage with amid the demands of early parenthood."

-Shushanik Karapetyan, LMHC

Licensed Mental Health Counselor
Certified Gestalt Therapist

"Sharon Itkoff Nacache and Yuliya Golubev have partnered on a down to earth guide to early motherhood chock full of creative ideas and inspiration. From thoughtful preparation to active help seeking and real life expressive tools, this book is a great companion for new parents."

-Gabrielle Kaufman, MA,LPCC,BC-DMT,NCC,PMH-C

Board Certified Dance/Movement Therapist
Licensed Professional Clinical Counselor
Certified Perinatal Mental Health Specialist

"Reading this book felt like Yuliya and Sharon were whispering the secret truths of postpartum directly into my ear. This book is a vital reminder that there is no perfection in motherhood, that we desperately need holding environments, that isolation is torture and that friendship is necessary. This book will nourish and support and guide you through the too often skipped over murky territory of what happens after we give birth. Consider it a gift from the postpartum angels."
-Jessie Kotler
Gestalt Therapist

"Yuliya's passion and insight into the world and minds of new moms is exactly what every new mom and perinatal practitioner needs to read. The passionate and empathetic words will help moms on their journey to becoming. Thank you Yuliya for your service to the women you graciously serve and protect. Thank you Sharon for your beautiful illustrations and prompts to work through what comes up for the reader."
-Jennifer Leopold, LCSW, PMH-C, IBCLC
Licensed Clinical Social Worker
Perinatal Mental Health Specialist
International Board Certified Lactation Consultant

"With compassion and a humorous touch, Yuliya Golubov pulls back the curtain on common challenges many caregivers face during the early days of motherhood. Along with Sharon Itkoff Nacache's vibrant illustrations and creative prompts, this book offers practical exercises for new mothers to claim their authentic experience."
-Gillian Lipton
Psychotherapist & Mother

"Yuliya Golubev offers a heartfelt examination of the good, the bad, and the messy that accompany the transition to parenthood. Her conversational writing style makes reading the book feel like getting advice from an experienced and wise old friend. Sharon Itkoff Nacache's creative prompts help readers integrate Yuliya's concepts with their own felt experiences, making the book feel even more personal. 'From Fantasy to Reality' is a digestible and practical manual for self-care during new motherhood."

-Adele Loux-Turner RSME, E-RYT 500

Pre/Post-natal Yoga Instructor
Infant Developmental Movement Educator (IDME)
Labor and Postpartum Doula

"'From Fantasy to Reality' is an insightful exploration of early motherhood, from the perspectives of two highly regarded therapists who intimately understand the mental struggles and emotional realities of new motherhood (that are glossed over too often). This book is an invitation to step away from rose-tinted motherhood myths, and feel seen, heard and understood during a vulnerable time. Yulia and Sharon offer a refreshing view into the often downplayed, though life-changing, transition into motherhood. They offer readers a sense of acceptance, understanding, and straightforward strategies to help navigate this fragile phase of motherhood. I highly recommend this book for anyone who is currently entering motherhood or contemplating becoming a mother. This book illustrates the mixed emotions that can flood us and offers helpful tools to navigate this period with illumination and ease."

-Julie Murphy, FNP-BC, PMHNP-BC

Family and Psychiatric Mental Health Nurse Practitioner
Menopause Society Certified Provider (MSCP)

"In From Fantasy to Reality: Real Talk on Early Motherhood from a Therapist Mom," Yuliya Golubev has provided new moms with a comprehensive understanding of the complex and contradictory experiences inherent in pregnancy and early mothering. As a teacher of attachment theory and a fellow therapist, I so appreciated Yuliya's ability to provide a safe and secure 'holding environment' for her readers. She offers support for all of the experiences intrinsic to new mothers, from trauma to joy, from impotence to acceptance, and she facilitates this task with humor, compassion and functional suggestions. I only wish that I had access to Yuliya's support and wisdom while enduring my own experience(s) as a first-time mom!"

–Connie Newman LMHC, LP, LCAT

Licensed Mental Health Counselor
Licensed Psychoanalyst
Licensed Creative Arts Therapist

"'From Fantasy to Reality" paints a very real and supportive picture of what it is like to become a mother. Yuliya references the common misconceptions and expectations people have that can lead to making the experience of new motherhood so much more isolating and harder than it needs to be, physically and emotionally. In making sense of the discrepancies between expectations and reality, she offers real, practical guidance for navigating it all with an abundance of compassion. Sharon's illustrations and creative prompts will further help you reflect and process your own beliefs and experiences more deeply, supporting greater self-awareness, and access to the best possible preparation for life after baby. I highly recommend this read for all parents-to-be."

–Yiska Obadia

Licensed Acupuncturist, Birth Educator, Bodyworker, Doula

"'From Fantasy to Reality'" is a compassionate, practical guide that gently bridges the gap between expectations and the lived experience of early motherhood. Blending therapeutic insight with accessible, validating reflections, Yuliya Golubev helps readers untangle the societal messages that can drown out their own inner wisdom, while Sharon Itkoff Nacache's thoughtful creative prompts make each short chapter easy to integrate into the realities of busy motherhood."

–Erin Spahr, LCPC, LCHMC, PMH-C
Licensed Clinical Professional Counselor
Licensed Clinical Mental Health Counselor
Certified Perinatal Mental Health Specialist

Author Acknowledgments

This book would not have been possible without my family's support, my parents, my kids, my grandparents, and my extended family. They inspired me with their resilience and creativity in life. This book would not have been possible without the support of my friends. I appreciate your reading my writings and sharing your comments and reactions. This book would not have been possible without the support from Gestalt Associates for Psychotherapy when I started my journey as a Gestalt therapist. My therapist, Michelle, my supervisors, and the whole faculty and community. Thank you for helping me believe in myself, learning how to be authentic and brave, and embody the good enough. Special thanks to Todd for teaching Winnicott's class, which inspired me to write about the good-enough mother concept and to embody imperfection. And a big thank you to my fellow mom and colleague, Sharon. Thank you for helping me with book editing, creating beautiful illustrations and creative prompts, and for holding my hand through this book journey. Because of you, I did not feel alone.

Disclaimer

This book is intended for psychoeducational and informational purposes only. It is not a substitute for psychotherapy, medical care, diagnosis, or individualized mental health treatment.

Reading this book does not create a therapist-client relationship with the author. If you are struggling emotionally, experiencing symptoms of depression, anxiety, intrusive thoughts, trauma, or feeling overwhelmed during pregnancy or postpartum, please reach out to a licensed mental health professional, your medical provider, or a trusted support person.

If you need perinatal mental health support, you can contact **Postpartum Support International (PSI)** for resources, support groups, and provider referrals: **www.postpartum.net**.

If you are in emotional crisis or need immediate emotional support, call or text 988 in the U.S. to reach the Suicide & Crisis Lifeline.

If you or someone else is in immediate danger, call 911 or go to the nearest emergency room.

Table of Contents

Introduction

Almost 20 years ago, I was pregnant with my daughter and had been living in New York for only two years, as a new immigrant from Belarus. Although it was a planned pregnancy and I had family support, I remember the first months of postpartum as a blur. The day blended with the night, and the night morphed into the day. What I experienced was not what I expected. I felt tired, lonely, and drained.

Since I was breastfeeding, I joined a local La Leche League group, met my La Leche League leader, and it was a game-changer. I started attending this meeting every Tuesday of the month at 11 am. I made my first mom friends and started feeling more confident as a mom. I no longer felt I was alone, and I finally had my circle of moms. I later transferred this experience to the local playground on Neck Road in Brooklyn, where I developed another mom circle. Our kids went to the local Russian day care together. I then found fellow mother friends with my younger son. And my professional home as a therapist is my Gestalt community at Gestalt Associates for Psychotherapy. When I opened my private practice, I knew who I wanted to work with: moms who feel lonely and overwhelmed and who feel a lot of pressure with too much parenting advice.

I decided to write this book because of my own early postpartum experience, my lonely feelings in early postpartum, finding a breastfeeding support group, La Leche League, making mom friends, and developing a mom circle of support here in the US. Last year, I started writing, and step by step, organized it into a book. As this was my first time writing, I reached out to my mom friends to do the "unofficial" quality assurance if what I wrote makes sense. I got lots of relatable reactions, laughs, tears, and everything in between, which inspired me to continue writing and speaking about the postpartum experience and its complexity, ambivalence, and absurdity.

As a parallel process to writing this book, I decided to practice what I preach. I did not want to write a book alone. I wanted to do it together with another therapist, who is a mom too. I reached out to my fellow mom therapist, Sharon, to collaborate, which enriched the experience. The rest is history.

For You, Dear Reader:

This book explores the postpartum period through the prism of my own experience and struggles. It is also written through the prism of my own privileges: having family support and being a white cisgender female. This book does not attempt to capture the full range of postpartum experiences. It is not a postpartum manual; it's honest, raw thoughts and reflections, and food for thought.

You may have heard the expression that there are different seasons of motherhood. Early motherhood, from the moment of conception on, is a unique season that requires so much of a mother. So it's only natural to need a lot in return. As you start reading this book, you will find that some chapters are more poetic and reflective; others are more practical and grounded. This is intentional. Some days you might need to feel seen or held, and other days you need practical advice on how to survive those seemingly impossible moments. Or maybe you need a good laugh or some creative prompts to inspire, reframe perspective, and help you get through. I hope this book provides you with whatever you need when you need it.

Warmly,

Yuliya

Mom, therapist, friend

PART I

The Myths and the Fantasy

Chapter 1
The Myths of Motherhood

Having a Newborn Is Easy: You Do Not Need Outside Help Or Other Myths Of Motherhood

- "Babies just eat and sleep, and it's the most beautiful and peaceful period of motherhood."
- "Our grandmothers didn't even have disposable diapers or all these fancy accessories – and they did just fine."
- "When the baby comes, you'll immediately have an instinct about exactly what to do.
- "This is the best phase of parenting, and you'll miss it someday."
- "You'll fall in love with your newborn instantly."
- "You don't need a nanny or any help; you'll learn how to do it yourself."
- You don't need any visitors or distractions during the first month."
- The baby needs a mommy, not a nanny."
- You're just exaggerating your fears about parenting."

Does any of this sound familiar, or maybe you've thought this yourself?

Welcome to the Myths of Motherhood.

We usually think of myths as old stories – the kind passed down through generations – stories that shape how we understand the world and our place in it. So the question is, how do these myths relate to our societal roles and beliefs about motherhood? What happens when we internalize these beliefs blindly to shape our expectations about what and how motherhood should be?

You might soon discover, as a mom, that...

- When your baby is crying, you feel the opposite of "peaceful or blissful."
- You find yourself lonely in your experience, and afraid to share darker feelings with family or friends for fear of seeming ungrateful or unfit as a mom
- You might be exhausted with the new role as a mother, but ashamed of asking for help because you wanted this and thought you could handle it
- Bonding with the baby does not happen instantly
- You might miss your old pre-baby life
- Or you might feel stuck in your home and want to see your friends or talk with the adults, not

about baby topics, but you might stop yourself from even entertaining these thoughts

In other words, you might have a different experience than you expected, compounded by feelings of loneliness in it due to societal pressure and norms. Let's start normalizing the idea that ALL different experiences have a place and all are valid. It does not mean you are a "bad" mom or that you do not love your baby. It also does not mean that motherhood is not for you or that you made a mistake by becoming a mom. Having rigid beliefs that are not part of your experience creates a sense of isolation and not being "good enough." But in fact, ambivalence is natural, normal, and even healthy in the complex world of motherhood. And bringing some self-compassion to your experience, along with outside support, gives you the energy and confidence you need.

Try reminding yourself: *My experience and feelings matter.* As you start to support yourself on your motherhood journey, you will begin to create an outline of your support system, both internal and external.

Where do these myths of motherhood come from, and what role do they play culturally?

One answer is that myths help us survive. To be clear, I am not making a historical claim here. I am writing about an archetypal story – the kind of story that gets passed from generation to generation and quietly shapes how we imagine motherhood and fatherhood. The archetypal myth might sound something like this... "Once upon a time, our ancestors lived in caves where the men hunted outside to provide for the family, and the women stayed inside to care for the children. The roles could not be mixed up; they had to be highly rigid to survive, and this narrative was passed down from generation to generation." Then came the parts about how motherhood is easy, beautiful, and natural. Any hardships or trauma was repressed and kept taboo. Mothers were seen as Martyrs who needed to be needless, since it was all about producing healthy heirs to the throne. Yet our parents, grandparents, neighbors, or strangers on the street have evolved beyond cave life, and survival instincts have adapted with them. If we give a voice to the ancient archetypal survival instinct, it will probably say, "I did it. You can do it. It is not so bad. Things could be worse." These myths of motherhood are deeply connected to survival. Remembering or recognizing the pain, exhaustion, and ambivalence of motherhood may have once felt too threatening, overwhelming, or confusing. Many lacked adequate support, and when ambivalence wasn't allowed, a simpler story became necessary: ***It was easy. I liked it. I managed. We need to continue our lineage, so you'll manage too.*** In a society that doesn't allow room for mixed feelings, this kind of story makes sense. When complexity isn't supported, people have little choice but to focus on a single acceptable emotion and push the rest aside. ***But motherhood is beautifully complex – and this kind of complexity deserves space.***

Creative Prompts

Reflect: What were some myths around motherhood shared among your family of origin while you were growing up? Were they spoken aloud or mostly modeled nonverbally through behavior or expectation? If you have siblings of a different gender, did they receive different messages? It may be interesting to explore this, alone or through conversation with loved ones.

Create: How does your personal experience differ from any picturesque fantasies you may have, now or in the past? Create a Fantasy vs. Reality Sketch by folding a piece of paper in half and depicting these differences, with your preconceived notions on the left side and current reality on the right. Collaging or scrapbooking work too, if you want to include pre-made images or sentimental 2-D items. Notice any areas of overlap as you add color and final touches. See if you can make space for both sides–literally on the page and figuratively within yourself.

Imagine: If a younger version of you were sitting in front of you now, what advice would you give her about new motherhood, knowing what you do at this stage? Notice your tone in how you approach her. Do you feel protective of her, jealous, or a different emotion? Try to hold all of the feelings that arise with compassion, as they are all valid.

Chapter 2

Maternity Leave: Survival 101

The Moment You Waited For a Long Time is Finally Here

You had your beautiful "surprise" baby shower at work, with tons of gifts and Martha Stewart-style delicious cupcakes. You're home, scrolling through pictures of the event, which took place last Friday, and it's now Monday. It's 6:15 a.m., and you still hear the alarm buzzing, so you turn it off. You no longer need to rush; take trains, be on time, and avoid meetings – you are free! **F-R-E-E.** You enjoy a quiet Monday, and your face breaks into a calm smile as you look forward to a peaceful maternity leave with all the time in the world to organize the nursery, take a stroll with your partner, and continue nesting. *Life is good*, you think, and then you feel a movement inside your stomach. You put your hand on your stomach and feel the baby moving.

Knock, Knock!

"Who's There?" Your Loss and Grief

Fast forward a week, and you are already missing your previously crazy, hectic lifestyle. You feel something is missing, though you cannot put a finger on it. The quiet morning without rushing no longer feels so calm.

Anxiety starts to set in – ***what's next? How will I give birth? How will I survive postpartum? How will I bounce back into my old clothes? How will I return to work? And who will I be without my work?*** That question shocks you: **Who *am* I *if* I *am not working*?** Even though carrying a child and being a mom is 24/7 work–the best and hardest job there is– just without pay, breaks, a 401(k), yearly reviews, or bonuses. Why does a strange feeling suddenly creep inside of you that you may miss your old life? You miss the meetings that used to frustrate you sometimes, the NYC commute with its delays and unpredictability, the rush to work, buying Joe Coffee and a fresh everything bagel with tons of cream cheese (which is not a healthy breakfast, but who cares). You miss ordering salad for lunch and not having time to eat it. Why, all of a sudden, are you not enjoying this quiet time and abundance of hours, but instead starting to feel scared?

Many Parents Feel Like You, especially in a productivity-obsessed capitalist society that values measurable outcomes over intangible, invaluable experience. What you're feeling is not strange, selfish, or wrong. You are not alone. Many parents are surprised to discover that alongside joy, there is grief. You may grieve the predictability of your old life, the stability of a paycheck, the comfort of coworkers (or even stress – yes, you may miss stress too), or even the "old you," the pre-pregnancy self.

This abstract feeling is called ***disenfranchised grief*** – the kind of grief that doesn't get recognized or validated by society. Everyone expects you to be glowing, grateful, and embracing every second of motherhood. The unspoken rule is: ***you should be happy, you shouldn't miss your old life.*** Your grief gets alienated, which might bring feelings of guilt and shame – that you are experiencing something "not right" – and you become scared to admit it.

In Gestalt therapy, we talk about ***introjects*** – those **"shoulds"** ***and*** **"musts"** we swallow whole from society: *You should enjoy every moment. You should not feel sad. Motherhood should be enough.* These messages can leave you feeling guilty or narrow the complexity of your feelings.

If you've ever wondered whether something is wrong with you for feeling excited and terrified at the same time, you're not alone. It is not only normal but healthy to feel this way because you are not just a pregnant woman or a mother; you are human too! – a surprise, indeed! As a human, you can have complex, ambivalent feelings. You can grieve the loss and also embrace the gain – pregnancy, motherhood, and everything that comes with it.

Survival Tips

Just like on a rainy day, the feelings of grief, loss, or anxiety during maternity leave can arrive suddenly. The question is not whether the rain will come, but what umbrella you have to protect yourself with.

It's better to prevent than to need treatment, just as it's easier to prevent isolation than to wait until you're in the middle of full-blown depression.

Here are some ways to be intentional about caring for yourself:

1. Make a list of resources:

Write down activities and places you can reach out to: La Leche League groups if you're planning to breastfeed, Mommy-and-Me classes, prenatal yoga, or neighborhood parent groups. *Repeat the mantra, parenting was never meant to be a solo activity – it has always been a village effort, and there is wisdom in that.*

2. Schedule activities that help you feel like yourself again

Book a hair appointment or a massage before you give birth, so you don't have to debate later whether you "deserve" it. Having it in your calendar makes it easier to follow through.

3. Be proactive

Ask friends to check in on you, or schedule visits. After you give birth, join a local playgroup and start exchanging words with other moms. Remind yourself that this is not a choice but a necessity to survive.

4. Talk to people near you

Go to the grocery store, have a little conversation with the cashier, or chat with the barista at your local coffee shop. Remember, you used to be a social person, not a monk in solitude.

5. Build small, predictable routines

Don't plan a trip to Hawaii just yet. Instead, create a rhythm you can rely on: Monday – Target, Tuesday – local coffee shop, Wednesday – take a walk with a local mom, Thursday – Whole Foods. Repeat after me: you are human, and humans thrive on connection and routine.

6. Remember: Isolating TOO MUCH is not nesting.

Solitary confinement has been used as a form of torture. That's how deeply isolation can impact the human mind. You have a choice to gently push yourself outside – even just a short walk, a chat with the barista, or a trip to the grocery store. Don't let yourself stay confined within four walls, as we are naturally social creatures who thrive on connection–even in the smallest exchanges. **You are Not and Do Not Have to Be Alone.**

Creative Prompts

Reflect: Close your eyes for a moment. How do you envision your time spent on maternity leave before the baby's arrival, beginning on day one? Now imagine a couple of weeks in what that might look and feel like. What do you notice in your body when you imagine this stretch of time? Feel free to journal your responses.

Create: Growing a human is hard work. Sleep can be disrupted during this time due to aches and pains. Jitters about unknowns and a growing to-do list can also make it difficult to slow down and rest. Channel that nervous energy by grabbing your favorite art supplies to create an Inner Peace Drawing. What evokes a sense of tranquility for you right now, or helps you to rest and restore? Try to represent it visually. After drawing, imagine or create a container for it where you can put your worries in order to get the rest you need.

Imagine a safe space for your growing family. What is needed to feel cozy and peaceful here? Is it indoors or an outdoor oasis? What colors do you see around you?

Do you notice any scents or sounds? Use your senses to visualize this scene, and if inspired, represent it with art materials of your choice. Note: If completing this exercise feels helpful, take a picture of it, print it out, and hang it up wherever you plan to give birth to use as a focal point.

PART II

The Reality

Chapter 3

"Baby Blues" and How to Manage Them

A question I often hear is what are the 'baby blues' and if it's the same as Postpartum Depression? They are often confused with one another, so let's first define them. Baby blues are prevalent in sixty to eighty percent of women and include symptoms of moodiness, sadness, irritability, and frequent crying. It often starts on the third or fifth day postpartum and is a hormonal response. What distinguishes baby blues from Postpartum Depression is the duration of the symptoms, as they often disappear on their own during the second or third week after giving birth, and can be accompanied by feelings of pleasure and calm in other moments. You might experience mood swings, be especially tearful and prone to crying, or more reactive than usual, and then after talking to a friend or partner or going outside, you start to feel better. Baby blues accompany several changes happening in a woman's body and environment, especially if she is discharged from the hospital several days after giving birth. This change in routine is drastic, with suddenly no help from nurses, unlike the support that may have been available in the hospital unit.

Copious milk production starts around this time, and you might also feel discomfort and hormonal shifts related to engorgement around early lactation. Pregnancy and giving birth create a rollercoaster of hormonal changes in your body and soul. Let's take a look at what happens to hormones after birth. Progesterone and estrogen decrease. Low progesterone is associated with feelings of anxiety and sadness. Estrogen contributes to the production of serotonin and dopamine, which help make us feel happy.

Second, ask for help. Asking for help is not easy, especially when you are a first-time mom. The societal message is that you are supposed to be happy and grateful to be a mom. There is no place for sadness and tiredness. Society has certain expectations about what it is like to be a mom, and social media only reinforces these rigid ideas. Not giving space or acceptance around what you are feeling might also bring a layer of shame to what you are experiencing. Asking for help is a skill. As you start developing new skills, you might feel discomfort, which is normal. Try to outline what kind of help you need to thrive. The help can be physical: taking care of the newborn (changing diapers, helping with feeding, doing the dishes, cooking, etc.). Help can also be emotional: asking your partner to check in on how you are feeling during the day, or talking to a supportive friend or family member who will validate your feelings without judging you.

Lastly, getting outside and moving can also have a drastic impact on how you feel.

Being a mom with a newborn can make even a simple task like getting outside feel like it's easier said than done. Depending on the season, dressing the baby in several layers can be more complex, especially if you are blessed with a more fussy baby. But it's worth it for the fresh air and the change of perspective. Despite all the difficulties and preparation, going outside, seeing other people, and seeing new surroundings rather than the four walls of your bedroom will shift your mood and reduce isolation.

Creative Prompts

Reflect: Have you ever experienced "the blues" before this perinatal period? What did that look or feel like for you? How did you get through it? Are any of those coping tools still accessible for you today? Feel free to write your responses in a safe place.

Create a Mood Boost Board that includes written words, collage, or hand-drawn images of simple, pleasurable everyday activities you enjoy, such as drinking tea, reading a book, enjoying a hot meal, washing your hair, listening to music, sending memes or texts to friends, etc. Keep it accessible for harder days when you need a visual reminder about all of the simple pleasures available around you.

Imagine: The power of compassionate affirmations has been proven to boost mood and lower anxiety. Are there any empowering or calming statements that have been useful to you so far in your family-building journey? Try to come up with at least three Personal Pep Talk Mantras. Ex: "This is exactly where I need to be right now, and I have everything I need within me." Note: *These statements can be helpful to write out, decorate, memorize, and/or practice at different stages of the reproductive journey, including labor/delivery and postpartum.*

Chapter 4

Motherhood Ambivalence: The Good, the Bad, and the Ugly

The Picture-Perfect Start

You did everything right—the baby shower, the glowing photos, the carefully researched stroller. You read What to Expect When You're Expecting twice and even highlighted the main points, hoping to memorize every possible scenario. You attended the classes, stocked the drawers with impossibly tiny onesies, and decorated a beautiful nursery with pastel colors and a mobile above the crib. You even posted your pregnancy pictures on the wall, proud and excited to step into this new chapter. You were ready – at least you thought so.

3 AM Reality Check: The First Signs of Motherhood Ambivalence

Nobody prepared you for the moment at **3 a.m.**, sitting in the dark with a crying baby, when a scary thought crosses your mind: "*Why did I sign up for this?*" You whisper to yourself, "*I miss my old life. I feel like an alien being a mom. I'm so exhausted. My nipples hurt. I can't even recognize myself in the mirror. My old clothes don't fit. I feel like a failure.*"

If any of these dark thoughts sound familiar, you are not alone.

Psychoanalysts have long understood what our culture still struggles to admit: motherhood isn't just bliss and picture-perfect moments. It's also exhaustion, resentment, and even flashes of hate–not of your child per se, but of the role and endless demand. And although psychoanalysis has its contradictions when it comes to women, one thing it got right was its vision of motherhood. It didn't romanticize it. It didn't sell us the image of a glowing mother gazing at her peacefully sleeping baby. Instead, it names the raw feelings you might be too scared, embarrassed, guilty, or ashamed to admit to your mom friend at the park.

Motherhood Resentment and the Ugly Feelings No One Talks About

Donald Winnicott, one of the most influential psychoanalysts and pediatricians, said something that shocked many when he first wrote it: mothers don't only love their babies – they also hate them. Yes, you heard that right: not only love, but hate. Not the kind of hate acted out in violence, but the everyday kind that mothers encounter and then hide out of stigma and shame. Every kind of feeling you might be too afraid to say out loud.

So, let's take a closer look at what Winnicott actually said about motherhood.

- Pregnancy itself puts the mother in danger, demanding everything from her body.
- Giving birth can be overwhelming, even traumatic.
- The baby immediately interferes with her private life and independence.
- Sometimes the baby is wanted more by the birthing parent's own parents or in-laws (if married) than by her.
- Breastfeeding can hurt – nipples raw, body aching, yet she is expected to endure.
- The baby is ruthless in his needs, treating her as an unpaid servant.
- At first, the baby has no awareness of what she has sacrificed.
- She must hold him calmly, without anxiety, even when she feels broken inside.

- And after a terrible night, the baby beams at a stranger, who gushes: "*Isn't he sweet?*" – while the mother herself remains invisible.

This is what Winnicott meant by a mother's "hate." Not cruelty. Not neglect. But the raw ambivalence of loving and resenting at the same time, especially when it calls on the mother to be a martyr and sacrifice her own comfort, is so common in early intensive phases. The complexity of motherhood goes far beyond the picture-perfect images we're fed.

Why Naming Ambivalence in Motherhood Matters

Winnicott writes that "a mother has to be able to tolerate hating her baby without doing anything about it."

What does that mean? It means that by being aware of the complexity of motherhood – the sacrifices, the toll it takes on your body and soul – you can begin to outline a path of support for yourself. If you are not aware of your ambivalence, of the mix of love and resentment, then you can't think about how to care for yourself.

It's like the rain analogy from the last chapter: if you don't notice the storm clouds, you won't bring an umbrella, and you'll end up soaked. But if you can name what's happening, you can prepare, protect yourself, and stay dry.

The same is true for motherhood. When you acknowledge ambivalence, you can begin to problem-solve what you need to tolerate it. Because motherhood is not one-dimensional, it is good, bad, and ugly – all at once. **And You Don't Have to Do This Alone.**

Creative Prompts

Reflect on the Postpartum Support Plan you have in place. This applies even if you are already in the trenches of newborn care, since it is for YOU as well as the baby. What did you envision for yourself in terms of daytime/nighttime help to share the blessing and burden of intensive early caregiving in terms of who will be doing what exactly, and when? If the baby is already here, it's never too late to begin to build your canopy of support if what you have in place is not enough. There is no shortage of experienced and compassionate childbirth educators, nannies, labor and postpartum doulas, night nurses, lactation consultants, perinatal therapists, pelvic floor physical therapists, acupuncturists, etc., ready to lend a helping hand.

Create a Mask by drawing a large oval on a piece of heavier paper like cardstock. Cut it out, leaving slits for the eyes and mouth if desired. On the front, sketch how you present yourself to the outside world using colors, lines, and shapes. On the back, represent how you are actually feeling on the inside these days. What do you notice, including how much effort you put into one side as opposed to the other? Both sides are representative of your current state, regardless of how they look to others, and it can be helpful to identify and externalize both.

Imagine yourself as a tree. What does it need to grow, especially during windy, cloudy, or cold days? Does it stand alone in a field or among a canopy of other trees? Now, consider your own resources–both inner (such as personality traits, talents, hidden superpowers) and outer (from my environment or community?) Based on this inventory, think about how you can support yourself in this new multidimensional role.

PART III

The New Mom in a New World

Chapter 5

Postpartum Anxiety: From Overwhelm to Calm

According to Postpartum Support International, one in five women and one in ten men experience anxiety during the perinatal period. These numbers might be much higher as many parents tend to suffer in silence due to the mental health stigma or societal pressure. Postpartum anxiety can either accompany or follow postpartum depression. Contrary to popular belief, it can also manifest anytime during pregnancy or the first two years postpartum. Postpartum anxiety has been getting more attention recently. You might experience these symptoms: constant worries, feeling that something bad might happen, racing thoughts, difficulties falling asleep even when the baby sleeps, not feeling hungry, or eating a lot. You might feel too scared to be alone with the baby or leave the house, worrying, having an anxiety attack, or feeling dizzy and light-headed. Postpartum anxiety can also accompany somatic symptoms such as having trouble breathing, chest pain, feeling trapped or panicked, feeling dizzy, and tingling or numbness in your hands or feet.

What causes postpartum anxiety? There are a lot of factors that can influence the amount or frequency of postpartum anxiety one experiences. For example, if you don't have sufficient support from a partner, family, or close friends, it can make everything much harder, especially if there is financial strain that limits how much you can outsource to others in the childcare or domestic sphere. Also, if you've gone through painful or traumatic experiences in the past or are predisposed to depression, anxiety, or other mood disturbances, that can impact how you cope after having a baby. Having complications during pregnancy or a traumatic birth can also increase your risk of having postpartum anxiety. Biological factors like having a thyroid imbalance can also impact how you feel. If you struggled with self-esteem or body image before becoming a mom, the postpartum period could also put you in a vulnerable place, feeling like you are not a good enough mom. If you experience systemic barriers—such as being a single parent, an ethnic minority, or part of an LGBTQ+ family—your stress levels may be higher due to a less supportive environment, stigma, and/or socioeconomic barriers.

When to Seek Help?

Postpartum anxiety can feel scary, overwhelming, and lonely, but you do not have to go through it alone and without support. The good news is that postpartum anxiety is treatable, and there is a path to feeling calm and peaceful in early parenthood. The question is, how do you understand when you need help? Whether you are a first-time parent or this is your third baby, it is normal to go through the adjustment period, feeling stressed and having some doubts. If the worries stay with you most of the day and impact your bonding with the baby or relationship with a partner, you notice that you constantly feel scared or stressed with no respite, or you start isolating yourself or avoiding certain everyday activities like being with the baby alone, getting outside, these are signs that more support is needed. As a perinatal trained therapist, my clients share how these worries can be paralyzing or all-consuming at times, which is why specialized support in this area exists.

Practical Strategies to Manage Postpartum Anxiety

1. **Acknowledge your feelings.** First things first, it's important to acknowledge what you are dealing with. Postpartum anxiety is a real mental health diagnosis and needs treatment and support, the same way a person with medical ailments would need treatment and specific routines. Of course, it's easier said than done; acknowledgement cannot be made in a vacuum; you need another human to validate what you are going through. It can be a therapist specializing in postpartum care, or a specialized support group for moms.

2. **Break the Cycle of Isolation.** Next, it is important to break the cycle of isolation. Anxiety loves four walls; anxiety thrives when we are alone with our thoughts, and anxiety wants us to think that our thoughts are the reality. Anxiety wants you to stay inside and hide your fears in an effort to protect you, but ultimately ends up serving the opposite purpose. Find a local support group, in person or online, peer or clinician-led, depending on what feels best. Postpartum Support

International offers many specialized free virtual support groups. You can ask your OB-GYN or pediatrician if they know of any local support groups.

3. Get Outside. Regardless of the season, try to get outside. Make sure you have a comfortable stroller with a rain cover or an easy-to-use baby carrier if you prefer. Remind yourself about the importance of going outside every day. You might not have the desire to go outside, and that's okay. Maybe it's the one outing you make daily, and that is enough. In the same way you remind yourself to brush your teeth so as not to get cavities, remind yourself to get outside, and how it helps to decrease anxiety.

4. Prioritize Sleep. The fourth thing is to prioritize your sleep. Rest while your baby sleeps. I know, I know, you've heard this many times, but you need to do your dishes, sweep the floor, do your laundry, and the list continues. Yes, you are right; your to-do list will not get smaller, and you can do all these house chores and feel sleep-deprived. As long as you are sleep deprived, that is what will make good conditions for your anxiety to grow. Try to prioritize your sleep. This may mean choosing a nap over doing the dishes, sweeping the floor, or scrolling through TikTok while your baby sleeps. The chores can wait; your sleep and recovery cannot.

5. Reassess Social Media Use. The last one is to try to re-evaluate the impact of social media on your anxiety. If your Instagram scroll brings you sadness, activates your inner critique, or makes you feel you are not good enough, that's important. If you find yourself comparing what you did with your baby throughout the day or how you look or feel to influencers, it's time to reassess this activity; whether they help you heal or escalate your anxiety. Remind yourself before going to social media that one in five women experiences postpartum anxiety, and what you just see is just a snippet of motherhood, but definitely not a full picture.

Creative Prompts

Reflect: Consider the role your anxiety is playing in the perinatal period: Is it protecting/serving you in some ways? Is it blocking or limiting your ability to function in the world or interact with others, or is it doing something else? Then consider what helps you feel grounded when you are nervous, and if you can implement a breathing, movement, or creative practice to help you through this period, such as the ones below.

Create a Daily Mandala Journal. Find or construct a small notebook where you can draw daily circles to doodle inside, depending on your mood that day. Mandala–meaning "circle" in Sanskrit–is an ancient archetypal symbol found cross-culturally in art and religion. Drawing mandalas and coloring inside of them on a regular basis can evoke a feeling of calm and wholeness, as they resemble the womb and face, the earliest nurturing forms we encounter in utero and birth.

Imagine your anxiety as a living, breathing being with color and dimension. If it had a name, form, and voice, what would it look, sound, or move like? What might it be trying to communicate? What does it need? How can you respond to it?

Chapter 6
Becoming a Mother Again

As a bilingual NYC therapist specializing in postpartum care, I've worked with many moms who feel overwhelmed, sad, or alone. This can make the prospect of starting the process all over again feel daunting, especially if there are unresolved issues from matrescence. Let's explore how you can rebuild joy and support for a reparative journey into motherhood, again.

What is Postpartum Depression? According to Postpartum International data, one in five women experiences postpartum depression. These numbers are probably much higher, as many moms choose to suffer in silence due to mental health stigma. As you may know from a first-hand experience going through a postpartum mood or anxiety disorder, its symptoms can feel quite debilitating. And yet, due to societal pressure, many birthing people do not get the help and support that they deserve. As you start thinking about having a second child, you might see this scary picture again: you are dealing with a postpartum mood disorder, and this time with an older child also demanding your attention. The good news is that although you do carry a risk if you have experienced postpartum depression previously, this experience can also serve as a pathway toward additional resources and support.

Remembering Your First Postpartum Experience

You might still have a pretty good memory of the scary picture that you experienced, recalling how postpartum felt overwhelming and lonely: how hours of the day felt so long, how you felt sleep-deprived, and how taking care of the long-awaited baby felt like a chore with no joy. You might recall how scary it was to stay with the baby, how getting outside with the baby felt like the "Mission Impossible" movies. Your pre-baby life felt like another universe, and you were an alien in it. You may have lost connection with your friends and felt ashamed to share what was happening with you. You forgot the last time you smiled or laughed. You might remember how much pain you felt, your tears on the pillow, and asking yourself a dreadful question: why did you sign up to be a mom? You remember looking in the mirror and seeing a stranger you hardly recognized. Or, perhaps you've repressed all of the gory details, but your body remembers, and you get a knot in your throat every time you think about expanding your family to include another child. Let's start with what we know.

What factors can minimize the risk of Postpartum Depression?

If you look back on your first experience of being a mom, what kind of support did you miss?

- Did you tend to lack internal support for your emotional needs?
- Did you have unrealistic expectations about what it would be like to be a mom?
- Did you compare yourself with the social media image of motherhood or new mom friends who seemed to "bounce back" so effortlessly?
- Did you rely on societal pressure about what motherhood should look like without checking in with yourself?

Isolation and the Lack of Support

The next question to ask yourself is whether you felt isolated or whether you had support. Did you rely solely on yourself to take care of everything for the baby and pride yourself on not needing help?

Did you make new mom friends, or did you stay in touch with your old friends?

Isolation tends to intensify the symptoms of postpartum depression. Postpartum depression often gets stronger when you stay alone with the baby for long periods of time. Depression also gets louder when you compare yourself to others and set unrealistic expectations that are hard to achieve when it comes to motherhood. Depression also grows when you constantly beat yourself up and criticize yourself. Isolation makes you miss out on hearing from another mom -"I've been there too". Isolation also makes you miss the chance to normalize your experience.

Joy and Self-Care

Another important question to reflect on is whether you experienced any joy while being a parent. Depression thrives when you stop doing things that used to bring you joy and help you feel good about yourself. Can you remember any simple, daily pleasures from that time period?

Asking for Help

Last but not least, did you ask for help?
Did you ask your family and friends for support?
Did you reach out for professional help, such as seeing a therapist who specializes in working with postpartum moms?
Did you have outside help with household chores?
Did you have a babysitter?
Did you allow yourself to reach out to a specialist who could help with specific challenges, such as a lactation consultant or a doula?

Looking Back to Move Forward

Reflecting on your first postpartum experience can be a powerful way to support and empower yourself as you prepare for motherhood again. By noticing what kind of support was missing, you can bring more awareness and intention to both external and internal support.

What does this mean in practice? It means beginning to bring awareness and support around postpartum depression. This might include joining a free support group through Postpartum Support International. Educating yourself and your loved ones about postpartum depression is key to recognizing it early and getting support sooner.

Know the Symptoms: Be mindful of persistent feelings of sadness, irritability, or hopelessness. If you notice these signs, don't wait—reach out for help. You can start reading books that talk about what you went through. Karen Kleiman wrote a book that focuses on Postpartum Depression, *This Isn't What I Expected: Overcoming Postpartum Depression.* Another great book worth reading is *What Am I Thinking: Having a Baby After Postpartum Depression* by Karen Kleiman, where she names the common yet taboo ambivalence around family planning as a PMAD survivor.

Build Your Support System

Support matters. Having people around you who can see you, hear you, and help you can significantly reduce isolation and emotional overload.

This might mean building or joining a mom circle—locally or virtually. Connecting with other mothers, sharing experiences, and hearing "me too" can make a real difference. Sometimes support begins with small steps: saying hi at the playground, asking another mom about a pediatrician, or starting a simple conversation that may grow into a connection. Remember to seek out folks who don't require extra effort to try to impress or perform for. A vulnerable, authentic connection should fuel energy, not drain it.

Support can also come from open communication with your partner, family, and friends. Let them know what you need—whether it's a listening ear, a walk together, help with meals, babysitting, or simply holding the baby so you can rest or take a shower. People often want to help but don't know how unless you tell them.

Professional Support Matters

In addition, consider what professional support might be helpful for you. This could include connecting with a lactation consultant, hiring a doula, or arranging reliable childcare so you're not carrying everything alone during the early postpartum weeks.

It's also important to let your OB-GYN or midwife know about any previous experience with postpartum depression. Having an open conversation about monitoring symptoms or considering medication options can be an important part of prevention.

Connecting with a therapist who specializes in postpartum mental health can provide tools, emotional support, and a safe space to process your experience. This kind of support can also help strengthen self-compassion, which is often deeply needed during this time.

Hey there, fellow mom! I know the thought of going through postpartum depression again can be really crippling. But remember, you're not alone, and this time you're armed with experience and awareness of resources available to you. This allows for the very real possibility of having a reparative experience, or an example of post-traumatic growth, where you feel stronger and more in control this time around.

Creative Prompts

Reflect: If you have had previous pregnancy and/or postpartum experiences, what would you do differently this time around? Notice which factors are within your control and which may be based on external or environmental variables. It may also be helpful to gently notice if any judgments are coming up around expectations you had of yourself or possible regrets.

Create a Mother Self Portrait using art materials of your choice, including old photographs if desired. Afterward, notice if you depicted her at rest or in action. Is she alone or surrounded by people and commotion? Consider what a stronger, "more prepared" mother of a new baby might look like and how she differs from your current perception of yourself as a mother, if at all. What might be missing, or could be removed? Go back to the original self-portrait and add or remove details to help make this maternal representation more comfortable, authentic, and/or fortified, such as pillows, fresh food, some good company, sunshine, etc.

Imagine: What scares you the most about expanding your family? Verbalize, doodle, or write the fear(s) down on a small piece of paper that you can fold up and eventually share with a trusted member of your support system. After sharing it, consider what you want to do with it: keep it in a safe place, discard it, or give it to them to hold for you?

Chapter 7
When Instagram Parenting Meets Real Life

It's already 10:57 p.m. You're drained after a long day, and your energetic three-year-old is bouncing on the bed, running laps around the apartment as if it's party time. You're already anxious about how your fifth-floor neighbors will look at you in the elevator tomorrow. You've done everything—took him outside, read the bedtime book, and offered endless hugs and kisses. And then the beautiful moment of parenting comes, the one you dreamed about when you were pregnant... I'm just kidding. Instead, boom! You lose your cool. You yell, "Go to sleep right now!"

I'm not saying yelling is good or desirable—what I'm saying is that when it happens (because it will), it doesn't mean you've ruined your child.

Where is all this gentle parenting now? Why, all of a sudden, do you feel more anger than patience toward your little one? Here's the truth: it doesn't mean you're a terrible mom. It means you're human. So welcome to the Imperfect Moms Club—not the Instagram Moms' Club. This is the club where moms occasionally lose their patience, yell, get tired, and (psst) sometimes don't even feel loving toward their child when he's still wide awake at 11 p.m.

You probably swore you'd never yell at your kids. You read dozens of parenting books and promised yourself you'd always stay calm and collected. Maybe you even had this judgmental look inside of you at the Whole Foods store when you saw a mom raising her voice at her kids. You swore you wouldn't repeat your parents' mistakes. Yet here you are. And the guilt hits instantly: "What have I done? Did I just traumatize my child?" Your mind races thousands of miles per hour into the future—you picture him years later in therapy, struggling with attachment issues because of this moment. The shame spiral gets activated.

You are facing an unpleasant reality. Not only did you yell, but you also failed to implement all the popular advice—"do this, not that," "gentle parenting hacks," all that blah, blah, blah.

And then the voice inside of you starts whispering: "You're a bad mom. Not only can't you put your child to sleep, but you're off the schedule, and you've probably harmed your child for life."

As both a therapist and a mom, I have some good news and some bad news for you.

The good news? Mistakes in parenting are not only unavoidable – they're essential. Yes, you read that right. Mistakes don't prove you're failing; they prove you're human. Not an AI parent following every rule from a book, but a real mom doing her best.

The bad news? Perfection in parenting doesn't exist. And chasing it will only leave you exhausted, ashamed, and further from the connection you actually want with your child.

The "Good Enough" Mother

This is exactly what British pediatrician and psychoanalyst Donald Winnicott meant when he coined the idea of the **"good enough mother."** A good enough mother adapts to her baby's needs most of the time, but not all the time. She comforts, soothes, and responds—but she also inevitably misses a cue, gets tired, or loses her patience. And those small moments of imperfection? They're what help a child learn that the world is not always perfectly predictable, that they can survive disappointment, and that they can grow their own resilience.

Yet, in my practice, I often hear a different story. Many of my clients carry such a loud inner critic that it completely takes the driver's seat. Whenever their parenting deviates from perfection, they retroflect—turning the energy of frustration inward against themselves. The retroflection is a Gestalt concept that means self-punishment. Parents see imperfection as a crime, and then the self-imposed punishment follows. They start blaming themselves, telling themselves what they did was horrible, terrifying themselves with catastrophic fantasies about the impact of their "crime" on their child's life.

Creative Prompts

Reflect on the patterns of your social media behavior with a reality check. Take note of who you follow and how they make you feel when looking at their content. Are you overloaded on gentle parenting advice or "trad wife" content? Could you use some more humor, reality, nature, or body positivity in your algorithms? Take some time to curate your feed in a way that feels nourishing, cleansing, and empowering.

Create a Talisman of Strength. Choose any special object (bead, charm bracelet, shell, stone, feather, or other found object) that can be a symbol of new parenthood, representing courage and resilience. Decorate it however you choose and put it in a safe place, or wear it on a day you need it most. Note: *Some prefer to use this as a literal touchstone to look at or hold during difficult moments to keep themselves grounded and centered.*

Imagine how you feel when walking into a fellow parent's messy home. Remember the smells, clutter, and smudges. Do you instantly judge them for the mess, feel empathy for the struggle, or maybe even secretly envy that they have surrendered to the chaos and let their home be in an imperfect but well-loved state for all to witness? See where you can embrace your own beautiful mess and sit with it. If you have a drawing utensil handy, try holding it in your nondominant hand and closing your eyes while you move it around on a blank page for 3 seconds. It may feel awkward or strange, and that's ok! Open your eyes and see if you can find an image within your doodle. Then use your dominant hand to bring out the representational image. Notice and appreciate what you've created when you were able to let go and trust the process.

Chapter 8
When You Do Not Feel Good Enough as a Mom

You thought you graduated from high school. You thought you survived college. You've been working for years. And then – boom – apparently report cards aren't a relic of the past. They show up in motherhood.

Welcome back to feeling not good enough, to feeling like crap, to comparing yourself and deciding others must be doing better. You didn't leave this behind in elementary school when you got a low grade on the spelling test. Nope. You've carried this lovely little gift right into your parenting journey

The Lovely Question

The number one question my postpartum clients hear from strangers, family members, even the cashier at Trader Joe's is this gem:

"Is your baby sleeping through the night?"

Usually, people ask it with a smile or with genuine concern on their faces. But here's the problem: this "innocent" question has the power to send your nervous system into overdrive.

You might notice butterflies in your stomach, tension in your chest, or sweaty palms. And most importantly, you no longer feel your passport age. You're seven or eight again.

You're sitting in elementary school. The teacher calls on you to answer a math question. Your mind goes blank. She gives you that judgmental look and says, "That's not good." Then she calls on another girl, who answers smoothly and gets praised.

And when someone asks, "Is your baby sleeping through the night?" those same old feelings show up. This is your motherhood test.

The Grade

An F? What? Because the truth is: your baby is not sleeping, not cooperating with the schedule. And you are exhausted – trying to implement family members' advice, scrolling Instagram posts, and desperately trying to catch up with those moms who seem to be getting A's.

The ones whose babies are "sleeping through the night."

Or at least that's what they tell you. Or what you hear. Somebody else is always doing better, and you are not doing enough.

Who's Handing Out the Grade?

So who is giving you the grade? The person asking you this question – or are you inducting yourself into this dynamic negative cycle? Motherhood just creates fertile soil for these old feelings, grading, and metrics.

The next question I hear from moms is: "What should I do??" – in a frantic voice.

The first thing: bring awareness. Notice that this is how you live in the world, how you relate to yourself and others. This isn't something new.

The person asking you the question suddenly doesn't feel like just that person. They might feel like your old elementary school teacher or your parent. And instead of being the adult with life experience and a career – and now also a mom – you shrink into the little girl who feels terrified of judgment and who hasn't yet learned how to support herself.

Validating the Little Girl Inside

So how can you see this little girl inside of you and validate her?

Tell her: *You are doing enough. You have the right to be here.*

Feel your legs on the floor.

Feel the stroller in your hands.

Notice today's date. Notice what year it is.

You are not back in that classroom. You are not seven years old. You are here, now – a mom, an adult, a human being doing her best.

Final Thoughts

My grandmother always used to say a Yiddish proverb: "*Why cry if we can laugh?*" Motherhood gives you plenty of reasons to cry – but sometimes laughing at the absurdity is exactly what helps you breathe. And if you've ever felt like you're getting graded on your baby's sleep, trust me: you're not alone, and you don't have to carry that shame quietly.

Creative Prompts

Reflect on your inner critic and how loud it may have gotten in this new, unfamiliar role. Try to drop into your body, close your eyes, plant your feet on the ground, and place one hand on your heart and one on your belly, or womb. With each inhale, breathe in and enjoy cooling blue breaths of gentle lovingkindness. With each exhale, breathe out red, prickly tension. Be sure to allow the exhale to be longer than the inhale to activate your parasympathetic nervous system and evoke a sense of calm.

Create a Love Letter to Yourself as a new mom. Sometimes the best way to listen to and eventually quiet the inner critic is to notice the unmet needs underneath and respond by mothering yourself with self-compassion. Get detailed in your letter to yourself and focus on small victories, silver linings, and areas of personal growth or resilience that have surprised or impressed you since becoming a mother. Talk to yourself the way you would speak to a precious, innocent creature or beloved soulmate.

Imagine the best qualities of your own parents, mentors, and primary caretakers in life. What does being taken care of feel or look like to you? What qualities do you hope to embody as a new parent? Use color, lines, shape, and texture to explore this concept.

Chapter 9

Learning What's Good for You: The Motherhood Decision Dilemma

“Sleep Training: To Be or Not to Be, That Is the Question”

If you ever dreamed about being on Survivor but never got the chance, don’t worry – your baby’s sleep training might just be your real shot to shine.

Days blurred into nights. You’ve finally hit your breaking point – picking up your screaming baby at 3 a.m. for the fourth time that night. A dilemma pops into your mind: *to be or not to be, that is the question.*

Exhausted but determined, you start researching. You ask ChatGPT about sleep training for a 6-month-old. You Google. You scroll through Instagram and TikTok. The more you search, the more flooded you feel by contradictory advice – and every piece seems to contradict the last. Suddenly, you’re too tired even to keep searching.

If, at the beginning of your search, you were trying to figure out how to do sleep training, by the end you found yourself Googling its impact on attachment styles. Suddenly, the price of a good night’s sleep seemed terrifyingly high: *anxious attachment, ambivalent attachment – what if I’m ruining my baby forever?*

"Forget it," you muttered, and crashed back into bed.

But of course, the next week arrived, and so did the same sleepless nights — and once again, a Shakespearean dilemma popped into your mind: *to be or not to be, that is the question.*

And just like that, you felt the existential weight of it all — despair, exhaustion, and the haunting question of life's meaning. Sleep-deprived, you wandered through your days like a half-alive zombie, wondering if this endless cycle would ever end.

Why Is It So Hard to Decide About Sleep Training?

So let's unpack why it feels so hard to decide what to do about sleep training — or whether to do it at all. The truth is, there isn't one perfect method or parenting philosophy. What you're feeling is completely normal: overwhelmed by mountains of information, expert opinions, and mom-blogger advice, all before you even have a chance to develop your own confidence and intuition about what's right for *you.*

And yes — I might disappoint you here. I'm not going to warn you about the "hidden dangers" of sleep training on attachment styles, or scare you about the "hidden dangers" of co-sleeping on your child's future sleep habits. I'm here to help you sort through the noise, build confidence in your own decisions, and trust that you are the best parent for your baby.

Bring It Back to Yourself

Ask yourself: *What does my family need? What do I need? What feels easiest and most comfortable for me right now?* These questions matter more than any expert debate.

And here's another tip: try to stick with one parenting philosophy at a time. Mixing two or three conflicting approaches will only drive you insane and leave you second-guessing yourself at 3 a.m. Consistency — not perfection — is what helps both you and your baby feel more settled.

Keep bringing it back to yourself. Ask: *What is my tolerance right now? What can I handle? What actually matters to me? What would make my parenting easier, not harder?*

As you stick to a parenting philosophy, keep bringing it back to **yourself** — to *your* needs, *your* journey, not to what an Instagram mom, your neighbor, or another parent is doing. Give yourself permission to keep reassessing how this parenting approach is working for you. Parenting isn't about perfectly following a philosophy; it's about choosing what fits your real life, your baby, and your values – and adjusting as you learn.

PART IV

Motherhood in the Real World

Chapter 10
No-Screen Parenting, Mom Shaming, & Fitting In

We all know about the danger of introducing screens from an early age – the effects of TV, the way a screen can become a free babysitter. My blog is not about that. I'm not here to *discover America* for you.

I want to dig deeper. Our choices of parenting philosophy – what do they really reveal about *us*?

My grandma used to say in Russian: «Всё хорошо в меру» (*everything is good in moderation*). I'm not suggesting you suddenly start introducing screens if you're doing fine without them. What I am saying is this: when the choice becomes rigid, it can make parenting more stressful than supportive.

Sometimes the "no screen" rule becomes less about our child and more about **fitting in with our mom friends**. If everyone around you is proudly "screen-free," it can feel like you'll be judged if you admit your child watches cartoons while you shower. And so the rule becomes about belonging – not just about development.

Maybe it's time to notice how much we shame ourselves when it comes to parenting choices, as if every decision carries the weight of a lifelong strategic plan. And if we judge ourselves too harshly, guess what?

We'll end up judging others the same way. Yes, screens are not for babies, the researchers are clear about the negative effects for young children. However, so is living in a polluted city, riding a train that damages your ears, or breathing air filled with toxins. If we only look at what's "bad for the child," we're missing half the picture: **the parent**. Because a constantly exhausted, shamed, and rigid parent can be just as harmful as a few extra minutes of screen time.

It gets depressing if we only tally up the dangers. Maybe it's time to notice the pressure we put on ourselves – and bring in more compassion and acceptance. Screens are bad, and yet turning on a show once in a while is not a criminal activity. We don't have to shame ourselves, and we don't have to shame other parents. In the end, what matters most is not perfection, but presence. A parent who can breathe, laugh, and offer warmth will always outweigh a rigid rule.

Creative Prompts

Try a Mini Digital Detox for yourself! Limit your social media consumption and spend some time engaging in creativity instead through guided meditation, journaling, or artmaking. Or, at least take a 5-second pause before reaching for your phone to begin scrolling, and do a short needs assessment based on the HALT acronym: Are you hungry, angry, lonely, tired?

Reflect: Will the digital device meet this need, or can it be met in real life somehow? What else can boost your dopamine levels?

PART V

The Mother's Body & Identity

Chapter 11

Getting Back to Your Body

You'd been waiting for that six-week postpartum check – honestly, even when you were still pregnant. You went to the gym. You looked at yourself in the mirror. You did not like what you saw – which is an understatement. Then you looked around – you were surrounded by fit women. A thought came to your mind: You need a plan. You need to really start working out, not just trying.

And then you heard this voice in your head:

No more bagel with cream cheese in the morning. No more lying in bed in the morning. No more excuses.

The voice continues: ***I do not care that you gave birth. Look around. Did you ever look at yourself in the mirror? You look fat. You really do.***

The voice almost started screaming and turned into yelling.

And you were standing and listening to this voice inside of you.

This voice sounded like a **Russian Olympic coach** – like in those YouTube videos where you saw athletes being yelled at, screamed at, and abused as they were trained to get a medal. Their whole life revolved around it – nothing else.

You looked around with energy and determination and found an empty treadmill. You started running. You soon realized that you were out of breath. The moment you stopped to drink some water, your inner coach started yelling at you: ***Stop making excuses! Show me your work! Do not stop! Faster, I said!***

As you listened to the coach and agreed with what they said, you made your best effort to start running again, but your body had a different plan and refused to cooperate with you or your coach.

Your body had a different voice: ***I'm tired, out of breath. I cannot run right now. I need some understanding — I gave birth to a human six weeks ago. I cannot perform under pressure.***

All of a sudden, you were confused about which voice to listen to. Your inner coach, yelling again, and you decided to try running once more.

You noticed that your inner coach's voice was louder and had more authority over your body. The inner coach treated you like an athlete, not a mom who just gave birth and is trying to work out. The inner coach was result-driven — faster, higher, stronger. The inner coach only used yelling, scaring, and shaming tactics to motivate you. And you were listening to this voice, almost agreeing with everything it was saying.

Then suddenly, you had an **a-ha moment**. You realized how often you give power to shame and pressure — and how little space there is for compassion, the reality of being a mom, and sustainability.

And then your body's voice took over, growing louder and louder, speaking the **truth**: *You are a mom. You just gave birth to a little human. You're taking care of a baby, which is physically and emotionally exhausting. You are not an Olympic athlete. You're a mom trying to figure out what's sustainable.*

As you listened to that voice, all of a sudden a feeling of warmth started to grow inside of you — a quiet sense of gratitude.

All of a sudden, you wanted to agree with this new voice inside of you — **you are fucking right! I *am a human. I am a mom. I am not an Olympic athlete. My body is sore, my breasts are leaking, I needed to pump an hour ago, and I didn't sleep last night or the night before.***

What happened to the Russian inner coach, you would ask? Did it disappear magically? No, the inner Russian coach did not disappear into nowhere. It was just a moment of movement and shift – aligning with a new part of you and noticing its impact.

Creative Prompts

Create a body outline for cultivating interoception and self-compassion. First, grab your favorite art materials to create a quick outline of a body, "gingerbread man"-style. Now close your eyes and do a brief body scan, beginning at the top of your head and moving your attention all the way down to your toes, taking a moment to pause at any muscles or body parts that you notice might be tight, holding, stiff, uncomfortable, or in pain. Now open your eyes and fill in the inside of the body, noting these special tender areas and giving them shape, texture, form, and color.

Reflect: We never ask the sky, stars, or ocean to take up less space. Why do we expect ourselves to be smaller instead of allowing ourselves, too, to expand with the ebbs and flows of life?

Chapter 12
Working From Home Burnout

The Marathon Before COVID

Remember, pre-COVID, you felt exhausted with the commute to the city, and it was only Tuesday. After work, you were running to Brooklyn to pick up your 3-year-old from daycare, then the race continued – home, kitchen, dinner, playtime, bedtime story, bath, brushing teeth. You collapsed on the bed, and you heard the Wednesday morning alarm. Sunday felt very anxiety-provoking – that the week and the race would start again. You also felt jealous of your friend who was working from home and did not have to run the NYC marathon as you did. This was your pace until COVID-19 and the shutdown.

The Shift During COVID

The COVID era brought shutdowns and survival mode – being a parent, employee, and teacher to your child all at once. Now your older child is back in school, but your little one is still tiny, and you've been working from home for more than four years. You notice the constant tiredness, the overwhelm from endless noise, and the juggling of Zoom meetings with the cries from the baby's bedroom. Being home all the time – never alone – has started to feel draining.

The Burnout Creeps In

Your sleep started to change – you found yourself scrolling late at night, struggling to fall asleep. Your appetite shifted, and your pre-COVID clothes no longer fit. A quick trip to Banana Republic to try on new pants left you disappointed when you realized you needed a bigger size. You also noticed how easy it was to stay in the apartment for a day or even two, and even when you walked your oldest to school, that short walk wasn't enough to move your body or clear your mind.

Why is that? You are not alone. What you've been experiencing are what we call the hazards of working from home. Many moms go through the same struggles and end up feeling burned out.

Hazards of Working From Home

Hazard #1: Blurred Boundaries

Working from the office often felt like a pain, but at least it had boundaries. There was a beginning and an end to the workday. There were breaks, lunch, chatting with co-workers, and even a trip to the office bathroom. The office had its pluses — including silence — compared to sitting in an NYC apartment at an 11 a.m. Zoom meeting and hearing your baby crying because she doesn't want to nap or just wants mommy.

The boundaries also included fully dressing up, putting on makeup, commuting, and not seeing your partner right after a meeting, or your baby rushing to hug you while you're working on an important deadline spreadsheet. The commute time was also its own kind of luxury — a chance to sleep, do your makeup, scroll, read a book, or just sit quietly. All of those small luxuries disappear when you're working from home.

Hazard #2: Isolation

I'm not telling you this to be dramatic, but remember that solitary confinement is used as torture in prisons for the most violent crimes. And while you are not a criminal, working from home comes with its own kind of isolation. You are cut off from co-workers, the NYC crowd, and even the quick trips to DSW during your lunch break. Gone are the casual chats in the office, the co-worker birthday celebrations at a restaurant, and the simple buzz of being surrounded by people.

Hazard #3: Your Body Feels It Before Your Mind

Your body began to show the effects of a lack of physical activity. You may have gained some weight because you're no longer taking the NYC subway stairs or running to catch the M14 bus before it leaves. The easy access to the fridge is another hazard your body does not appreciate. And your body is also tired from the constant noise – your baby crying, your partner talking, the nanny moving around.

Hazard #4: Emotional Drain

You notice yourself scrolling more and finding it hard to read a book or to focus your attention. Your eyes are tired from endless Zoom meetings. It's hard for you to sit still. You don't have the alert mornings you once did – instead, you wake up later and rush straight to your laptop. You might forget to have breakfast or even sip your favorite ginger tea. Every day feels like one long blur, melting into the next, never really ending.

Survival Tips for Moms Working From Home

You've been burned out from working from home. So what are some survival tips?

1. Create a Routine

Wake up earlier. Do some body stretches or walk around the block. Have breakfast in your kitchen, not during a Zoom meeting. Start putting this routine in your Google Calendar.

We are human, and we are creatures of habit – whether you graduated from the Ivy League or not. We thrive on routines and predictability. Start creating small routines with a clear beginning and end.

Have lunch in a designated area – it's called the kitchen, not your desk. Put away your phone while you eat. Notice what you're eating: the texture, the smell.

You've been multitasking for too long. You deserve some time to slow down and do one thing at a time.

2. Prioritize Moving Your Body

Commit to moving your body as part of practicing mental hygiene. The same way you practice brushing your teeth daily to prevent future cavities, remind yourself of the importance of moving your body to take care of your stress.

Have you ever thought about why we sit in a therapy session? When we sit, we get in touch with our feelings. At the same time, when we start moving, we feel less stuck in our thoughts and more connected to our bodies. Moving creates a rhythm that helps you to feel safe, helps your brain to lower the stress.

When you can, try to get outside. Getting outside creates a more beneficial effect to lower stress. It helps you to get out of your head and notice what is around you. What works for a crying toddler might magically work for you. If your child is cranky, you might try to distract them with a toy, book or getting outside. Distraction helps the child to focus on something else. Same as us. Try to get outside.

Believe it or not but I love to get outside when it's rainy. I am not talking about the thunderstorm of course. I love feeling the raindrops on my hands and my face as it creates a sensory experience and helps me get out of my thoughts. I also love the sound of the rain. Buy a cute raincoat in the color you like. I love the Columbia brand, the light purple one.

3. Be Intentional About Scheduling Time With Friends and Co-Workers

Yes, it feels forced – but it has to be. You're no longer running into co-workers in the office kitchen or grabbing a spontaneous happy hour with friends after work. That casual connection is gone when you work from home.

So you need to reach out and make the plan. Text your friend, schedule the coffee, suggest the walk. Most of the time, they'll be happy to say yes – because if they also work from home, they're probably struggling with the same challenge you are.

The challenge is real. The struggle is real. So don't wait for the connection to "just happen." You have to create it.

4. Start or Resume a Hobby

I will not tell you to stop scrolling – because before you quit, you need something to trade it off with. The truth is, scrolling fills a gap. So experiment with your hobbies. Try your old ones again and notice how you like them now. What kind of energy do they give you? How does your body and soul feel after doing them? Then, try something new. Give yourself the chance to replace mindless scrolling with something that actually feeds you.

5. Postpartum Sleep Hygiene 101

Do not look at the clock if you can't fall asleep. If you can't fall asleep, don't lie in bed tossing and turning for an hour. Get out of bed and do something dull, like reading. But don't do it in bed. Do not forget to nap during the day if you had a bad night of sleep or your baby did not cooperate.

Chapter 13

Going Back to Work After Maternity Leave

Those early days with a newborn felt so slow, even monotonous at times. But the nights blurred into days, and somehow the weeks of maternity leave vanished far too quickly. Suddenly, you found yourself facing a new chapter: preparing to return to work. **Along with the practical logistics, you might notice a mix of emotions – excitement, guilt, anxiety, and even grief -sitting inside you and talking at the same time, interrupting each other.**

You might start thinking about going back to work much earlier than when your maternity leave officially ends. Many women find themselves missing the identity they had before the baby was born – being in the office, chatting with colleagues, having an uninterrupted lunch, or even the rhythm of a daily commute, being fully dressed, having showered, and having full makeup. When you are dealing with the newborn, these things feel like luxuries or your alien identity. If your work was once a source of joy and connection, you might long for those parts of life.

For others, the relationship with work looks different. Maybe your job felt like a source of stress and expectations, and the idea of returning leaves you feeling drained. Or if you had a stressful boss, an unsupportive team, or a terrible commute, you might actually feel overwhelmed by adding going back to work to your already full plate.

The truth is, going back to work after maternity leave is rarely just one thing. It's more like a rainbow. A rainbow does not include just one color – it's the presence of many colors together. In the same way, returning to work can bring a blend of feelings: excitement about adult conversations and reconnecting with colleagues; fear of leaving your baby; the hassle of childcare and breastfeeding logistics; the challenge of juggling two shifts (work and home); and the relief of having something beyond motherhood. All of it can coexist.

I remember when I got back to work, I was sitting in the office and thinking, "It cannot be true that it's already so good to sit in the quiet space and not be overstimulated, and they will pay more for that!!" But that's my experience, your experience matters too!

5 Tips for Returning to Work After Maternity Leave

1. Lower Your Expectations

This transition is huge – and it's normal to feel overwhelmed. Remind yourself that your "workload" now includes three full jobs: adjusting back to work, caring for your child, and managing your own recovery. You can't (and don't need to) do it all perfectly. Your plate will already be full – adjusting to work, managing childcare, missing your baby, and figuring out breastfeeding or a pumping schedule. That means your stress level may be higher than usual.

Because of this, it's important to prioritize what matters most and make some things secondary. For example, if your focus is adjusting to the rhythm of work and managing the emotions of being away from your baby, then house cleaning may need to take a back seat or be delegated to someone else.

Take a moment to notice what thoughts and expectations you hold about going back to work. What do you expect from yourself? And where do these expectations come from – your culture, your family history, social media, or your own inner critic?

Sometimes it helps to imagine a friend in the same situation. What would you suggest to her if she were preparing to go back to work? Would you encourage her to give herself grace and flexibility? Now ask yourself: are you offering the same kindness to yourself, or do you hold yourself to a harsher standard?

2. Notice Your Inner Critical Voice

Your inner critic might whisper that you're a "bad mother" for going back to work and leaving your baby with a nanny or in daycare. But that voice doesn't always see the full picture. The full picture is that you might not have a choice or the luxury of not returning to work, or you might not be living in Sweden, where maternity leave is long, and you might need to provide for the family. Or the full picture is that your choice to go back to work is for your mental health, or because your career is important to you.

3. Simplify, Simplify, Simplify.

"Simplify, simplify, simplify" can become your survival mantra. If you're breastfeeding, keep a second pump at work so you don't stress about forgetting it at home. For meals, delegate when possible, or cook simple dishes in bulk and freeze them. These small adjustments free up energy for what matters most. When you come back to work after a long commute, do not try to be Maria Montessori by doing arts and crafts or trying a sensory play activity you saw on Instagram from another mommy influencer. Just do not do it! Your baby will not say thank you to you, but you will find yourself super exhausted. Instead, cuddle with your baby, bring a cozy blanket, and read a book. That's more than enough. What is more important, these activities will not drain you and will be gentle with yourself, rather than putting more pressure on being a mom.

4. Lean on Your Village

This is not a time to go it alone. If you're breastfeeding, talk to a lactation consultant about how to make breastfeeding easier while you're going back to work. Schedule a coffee or check in with a mom friend who has also returned to work. Share survival tips, bring humor to sleepless nights, and remind each other that nobody has it all figured out. Vulnerability builds connection. By normalizing the struggles, you can quiet the inner critic and avoid spiraling into "bad mother" versus "bad employee."

5. Keep Making Time for New Mom Friendships

Even after you're back at work, continue building connections with other moms. Join a local Facebook group or sign up for a "mommy and me" class – swimming, music, or a playgroup. These spaces help you form friendships with moms who understand the challenges firsthand. Join a local Yoga studio or Pilates studio. These are great places to make connections. Staying connected in this way strengthens your identity as a mother while also reminding you that you are not alone in the ups and downs.

Final Thoughts

Going back to work after maternity leave is not about doing it perfectly – it's about finding a rhythm that feels sustainable. Remember: you don't need to be the ideal employee and the perfect mother at the same time. Being "good enough" in both roles is already more than enough.

PART VI

Connection and Building Your Support

Chapter 14

Being Held: The Power of Your First Circle

I was feeling so angry on a recent Wednesday morning. I asked my mom's friend, who goes to a well-known pediatric office, if she could bring the flyer for a postpartum support group for new moms to the office.

The response I heard really enraged me. Apparently, there is no way they can just bring a flyer about local providers who are helping moms – it has to be mailed to the main office for approval.

The office is famous for its "excellent" pediatric care. But what is excellence when it comes to being a pediatrician? Of course, making the right diagnosis is important – but what about mothers' mental health?

The culture makes referrals difficult, and local providers are not well-known. What "excellence" are they talking about? It reminds me of the place I came from – a communist country. We had loud mission statements on paper, but people suffered in silence. There was a hush culture around mental health – and God forbid, especially maternal mental health.

Moms were supposed to be happy, grateful to be mothers, and self-sacrificing. Pediatricians were the "experts," often shaming moms. So we are back to my childhood. Why is it 2026, and maternal mental health –

including the mother's need for a circle of support – is still not part of what we call excellence in baby and mother care?

Is the system built to gaslight and hush maternal mental health? Yes, it's sadly true. Apparently, even connecting with a local circle of moms now has to be approved by the "experts from above." Pediatricians can't make their own decisions; they have to consult. Wow. I'm speechless.

Does child mental health really matter? How can a child's mental health be separated from the parents?

In this moment of rage, I also want to acknowledge the **"old-school pediatricians."** I remember when I was dealing with early postpartum struggles, I joined a **La Leche League** group, and the leader gave me a flyer about the group to share with my pediatrician. My pediatrician was very appreciative of this information. Her office was in the basement, and she did not have loud mission statements or a patient portal. She was listening to her intuition, as she was not only a pediatrician but also a mom and an immigrant. A few months later, another Russian-speaking mom joined the group, and long story short, we became best friends

– and our kids became best friends. I joined the **La Leche League of Brooklyn- Marine Park/Madison**– and my local La Leche League leader (if you know this phenomenal woman, mother, the leader – if you know, you know) became more than just breastfeeding support. We developed a beautiful friendship that's now 20 years long and counting!! That's how it's supposed to be! So yeah, when I joined the La Leche League. I wasn't just a new mom – I was also a new immigrant, having only been in the U.S. for three years, trying to navigate motherhood in a country that wasn't my own, without a single local mom friend.

I also want to recall the famous pediatrician, mother advocate, and psychoanalyst – **Donald Winnicott** – who hosted a popular radio show about parenting from 1943 to 1960. He emphasized the importance of a **"holding environment"** for mothers to provide optimal care for their children. What does "holding environment" mean in simple terms?

Think about a mom in the nursery. The baby is crying. The mom hears the cry and rushes to pick up the baby. She holds the baby and tries to figure out what the baby needs – is the baby hungry, needs a change, lonely, or overstimulated? She tries intuitively to soothe the baby. But first things first – the cry is real and needs to be addressed.

Now think about the pediatrician and the postpartum mom. The mom's exhaustion, isolation, and stress are important and need to be addressed. So, what about the tired new mom in the pediatrician's office? Is she allowed to voice her needs and be heard? Or do her needs not matter?

The baby learns that they can cry and that they are allowed to express their needs; if ignored, they may learn that crying doesn't bring any change, as with babies in orphanages or institutions. They learn to cry quietly or stop crying altogether because nobody cares. When I attended my **local La Leche League breastfeeding support group**, I unconsciously felt "held." Jen has been a great and kind host, she was always making the famous delicious vegetable bagel spread (if you know you know), she was always making sure moms eat, and she was helping moms with simple but so important tasks- holding a crying baby while moms eat, teaching moms how to use slings. I remember we talked about everything from sore nipples to MIL, baby sleep, intimacy after postpartum, society standards, and moms were just talking freely. We laughed together and cried together. I truly believe this group saved me from developing postpartum depression, and this group became the anchor of support and, more importantly, a circle of mothers in the new country. And now, almost 20 years later, I want to give back to new moms what I got from Jen-I want to run my own postpartum support group for new moms. A group where new mothers can feel held, seen, supported, and connected.

Maybe my anger this morning wasn't just about one flyer. It was about the silence that still surrounds mothers. The truth is, every system needs to learn what good mothers already know — when someone cries, you don't send it to headquarters for approval. You listen.

You don't need a Joe from upper management to tell me that what I'm doing "needs to be approved." We deserve to be seen, heard, and held — just because, not when another upper party decides.

Chapter 15

Making Mom Friends: The Internal Obstacles

The Lonely Side of Motherhood

Many new mothers share with me their profound sense of isolation. One of the most common goals I work with moms on is helping them develop connection—mom friends. Mom friends can provide an amazing sense of support in normalizing the postpartum journey and its challenges, and a place to share the highs and lows of motherhood. Having mom friends can be a valuable resource to prevent postpartum depression.

Making Friends Isn't Rocket Science — So Why Is It So Hard Now?

Making friends isn't rocket science. You've done it before — in kindergarten, in the high school cafeteria, or in the first months of college. You already know what to say and what to do.

So I'm not going to waste your time giving you a script for small talk. What I hear most often from my clients isn't about what to say — it's about the internal barriers that make it hard to reach out, be visible, offer friendship, or maintain one.

The Barriers to Connection

Barrier #1: Fear of Rejection

Ta-da!! You guessed it: the oldie but goodie – fear of rejection.

As a mom, you might feel scared to take the first step because you worry about being judged or dismissed. Maybe another mom will critique your parenting style, your look, how quickly (or not) you're "bouncing back," how your baby sleeps, how you feed your baby... and the list goes on.

Fear of rejection doesn't just come from the present moment. It carries echoes of the past – old experiences of not feeling accepted. In Gestalt therapy, we look at how these old voices live in us now and how they can stop us from reaching out.

Barrier #2: Comparison

If fear of rejection wasn't enough, along comes its close cousin – comparison.

You meet another mom at the playground and suddenly notice everything she seems to be doing "better." Maybe her baby sleeps through the night. Maybe she looks like she bounced back effortlessly.

Maybe she talks about her supportive partner while you're barely keeping your head above water.

Comparison sneaks in fast, and social media makes it even louder. We end up stacking our messy, real-life insides against someone else's polished outside.

From a Gestalt perspective, comparison often hides a deeper truth: it's less about the other person and more about the parts of ourselves we struggle to accept.

Barrier #3: Exhaustion & Overwhelm

Sometimes the biggest barrier isn't rejection or comparison – it's just pure exhaustion. In the postpartum months, every ounce of energy goes into feeding, changing, soothing, and maybe sneaking in a shower. The thought of putting on real clothes, packing a diaper bag, and meeting another mom can feel like an impossible task.

Clients often tell me, "I want friends, but I just don't have the energy to invest." And that's real. In Gestalt therapy, we'd say your energy is "tied up" in survival tasks. Until you reclaim even a small pocket of space for yourself, reaching out can feel like another impossible demand.

Barrier #4: Avoidance ("I Had Friends Once... But Not Anymore")

Another quiet barrier I hear a lot in therapy is avoidance. It sounds like this: "I had close friends in the past – in high school, in college, at my first job. But now? I'm too old. I don't have the energy. Real friendships don't happen anymore."

Avoidance shows up as that inner story that convinces you it's not even worth trying. Sometimes it comes from grief – missing the ease of friendships that used to form naturally. Sometimes it's a defense, a way to protect yourself from the risk of being let down.

From a Gestalt perspective, avoidance is a way of pulling back from contact. It feels safer in the moment, but it also cuts you off from the possibility of a new connection. You end up reinforcing the very loneliness you long to escape.

The truth? Friendship doesn't have an expiration date. Yes, it looks different after kids – there's less time, less spontaneity – but the human need for connection doesn't go away.

What Helps?

So now that we've named some of the big barriers – fear of rejection, comparison, avoidance – the question becomes: what actually helps?

The good news is, making mom friends doesn't require magic or perfection. It's about taking small steps, noticing your inner voices, and allowing connection to grow in its own messy, real way.

1. Notice the Inner Voices

Remember those barriers we talked about? The fear of being judged, the comparison spiral, the "I'm too old" story? Those are voices, not facts. In Gestalt therapy, we talk about the power of awareness. When you notice the critic saying, "Don't bother, she won't like you" – pause. Ask yourself, "Is this really her voice, or is this my old inner critic talking?" Naming the voice gives you a choice about whether to listen to it. Try to build a relationship with that voice. Try to understand what this voice is trying to protect.

2. Make Efforts

Remember when you were living in the dorms – making friends did not feel effortless; it was just the natural way of breathing. When you become a mom, you need to make efforts to show up in places where you can see other parents. Friends do not come to your Manhattan apartment, knock on the door, and say, "Please open, this is your BFF waiting for you." No, you will have to make efforts and be intentional.

Join the local La Leche League if you are breastfeeding. Join local Facebook groups for parents. Join local mommy-and-me classes. Join the YMCA family swim – these are great places to show up and initiate conversation.

3. Stay Curious

Remind yourself to stay curious the next time you haven't seen a text reply from your mom friend. Rather than going to the familiar narrative "She does not like me," remind yourself that you do not know what is going on with her. Tell yourself, "I am curious why she did not respond," rather than, "I know why."

4. Take Risks, Be Vulnerable

Think about your BFFs. What is the common denominator between them? Bingo – you can be yourself without filters. Now the million-dollar question: did it start this way? Hell, no.

Remember the first time you had to inhibit yourself and, over time, shared with your friend your darkest secrets – and she still accepted you for who you are. The same applies to mom friends. Start testing the waters. Share something more or less vulnerable and notice their reaction. If it's safe, share more. Without risk, friendships stay surface-level.

5. Show Up

Showing up is hard – but it simply means leaving the house with your baby. Yes, I know, I know, it's not easy, and you have to prepare around the baby's schedule. But trust me, the more you do it, the easier it gets. Go to the local playground. Take a stroll in Prospect Park. Go to the local mommy-and-me. Attend a story time at the **Brooklyn** or **Manhattan libraries**. Buy a membership at the **Brooklyn Children's Museum** and a family pass to the **Brooklyn Prospect Park and the New York Aquarium**.

Chapter 16

Daycare: The First Separation

You did your thorough research. You asked your mom's friends. You asked the Facebook groups. You had a tour of the daycare that was highly recommended. You were impressed by the teachers – warm, patient, and caring. The space felt safe and inviting: bright colors, soft rugs, tiny tables and chairs, shelves filled with plush animals and little toy cars, a cozy reading corner with picture books lined in a row. Everything looked clean, organized, and cheerful. You felt excited and good about your decision – your little one will start daycare!

The month passed by very quickly. You prepared the long list: sleeping mat, an extra pair of clothes, a sippy cup, diapers, hand sanitizer, and several pairs of socks. You decided that you would be the "designated driver"-you will be taking your little one on the first day.

You put your son in the stroller. The moment you started walking toward the daycare, you began feeling butterflies in your stomach – the same way you feel when you're scared. The tummy sensation grew bigger and bigger, then jumped to your chest, making it difficult to breathe.

You opened the door, handed your son over, and he started crying hysterically. Although the teachers were trying their best to soothe him, you were terrified by how loud his cry was.

You rushed to the Parkside Avenue station. You hopped on the Q train. And all of a sudden, instead of the relief and excitement you were expecting, you started feeling tears you tried to suppress – after all, you had just done your makeup and had a 10 a.m. meeting with your team. But the tears had a different plan. They didn't want to play hide-and-seek. You felt a lump in your throat. All of a sudden, it was hard to breathe.

You realized you couldn't suppress it anymore, so you camouflaged by wearing sunglasses – so you could cry on the train without anyone seeing.

"The next stop is DeKalb Avenue, please stand clear of the closing doors," you heard – and that's when it started pouring really hard. You took out your phone to distract yourself, scrolling through unread messages and Instagram updates.

As the day went by, you got your first update from the daycare – a picture of your son sitting in circle time. Your heart melted. He looked so cute, and you felt a rush of joy and pride. He was wearing his Old Navy sweater and sweatpants. He looked happy. You sent the picture to your partner. You felt good about this milestone.

All of a sudden, you noticed you didn't have a lump in your throat anymore. You were breathing. You felt another rush of joy. You started forwarding the picture to your mom, your friends, and your in-laws. Hearts and likes started pouring in.

At lunchtime, you went out with your best friend, who is also a mom. You vented about your first drop-off, and she said, "Yes, I felt the same." All of a sudden, you felt comforted. You talked nonstop about your ups and downs on the train ride, showing her the cute picture of your son. You noticed her smile—and a little sadness in her eyes — when you described your tears that refused to cooperate.

The day passed quickly. You rushed to the 23rd Street station to catch the R train, then transferred to the Q at DeKalb Avenue. You heard again, "Please stand clear of the closing doors." But this time, you weren't wearing sunglasses to hide your tears. You felt excitement in your chest — to see your son again and ask the teacher a million questions.

When you got off at Parkside Avenue, you were almost sprinting to the daycare, despite not running a marathon. You opened the door. You saw your son on the teacher's hip, cuddled close while she sang a song. Your heart melted again.

All of a sudden, your son saw you and started reaching his arms toward you, saying, "Mama." This was the moment you had waited for all day – like a slow-motion movie – his little run toward you, your hug. The teacher gave you a detailed report: how long he napped, what he ate, and how he slept. Everything sounded more than kosher.

You decided not to put him in the stroller – instead, you carried him while pushing it. You felt the warmth of his body, your breathing syncing together. You were crying again on the street, but this time you weren't hiding your tears. They felt like tears of reconnection – tears of joy.

Daycare is more than a practical decision – it's a symbolic separation. It carries with it layers of grief, fear, and longing – not only for the child, but for the mother too. Both are stepping into something new: the child into a world beyond home, and the mother into a life no longer defined only by constant closeness.

But when the environment is supportive, the separation becomes bearable. The caring teacher who gently sings while soothing the crying child, and the mom's friend who listens and validates her tears – they both create what Winnicott called a ***holding environment:*** an emotional space that allows both mother and child to fall apart a little and still feel safe enough to keep going.

In these moments, the importance of the holding environment becomes so clear. The baby needs someone who can stay calm, attuned, and present – a teacher who can hold their tears without fear. And the mother needs that too. She needs a space where she can cry, laugh, and be understood without being told to "enjoy her freedom" or "get over it."

That's what I think about often in my work with mothers. Therapy, too, is a kind of holding. I listen. I laugh with them. Sometimes I share their sadness. Through this mirroring, something softens. They begin to feel seen – not as someone who should have it all together, but as a woman who is human, feeling, and growing alongside her child.

Because when we are held — truly held — we find the courage to hold others.

References

Kleiman, K. R., & Raskin, V. D. (2013). This isn't what I expected: Overcoming postpartum depression (2nd ed.). Da Capo Lifelong Books.

Postpartum Support International. (n.d.). Postpartum Support International. https://www.postpartum.net/

Winnicott, D. W. (1945). Primitive emotional development. In Through paediatrics to psycho-analysis: Collected papers (pp. 145–156). Hogarth Press.

Winnicott, D. W. (1947). Hate in the counter-transference. In Through paediatrics to psycho-analysis: Collected papers (pp. 194–203). Hogarth Press.

Winnicott, D. W. (1956). Primary maternal preoccupation. In Through paediatrics to psycho-analysis: Collected papers (pp. 300–305). Hogarth Press.

Winnicott, D. W. (1958). The capacity to be alone. In The maturational processes and the facilitating environment (pp. 29–36). International Universities Press.

Winnicott, D. W. (1986). The theory of the parent-infant relationship. In P. Buckley (Ed.), Essential papers on object relations (pp. 233–253). New York University Press. (Original work published 1960)

Winnicott, D. W. (1986). Transitional objects and transitional phenomena. In P. Buckley (Ed.), Essential papers on object relations (pp. 254–271). New York University Press. (Original work published 1953)

About the Author

Yuliya Golubev, LMHC-D, LPC, is a bilingual (Russian-English) psychotherapist, certified Gestalt therapist, and mother of two. She immigrated to the United States from Minsk, Belarus, in her early twenties, and her experience of immigration and living between cultures continues to deeply inform both her life and therapeutic work.

Prior to opening her practice, Yuliya has worked in a wide range of mental health settings across New York City. She opened her private practice in 2017 and currently sees clients in her office in Brooklyn Heights, New York. She also completed a four-year clinical fellowship in Gestalt therapy at Gestalt Associates for Psychotherapy, which continues to shape not only who she is as a therapist, but also who she is as a person.

Today, Yuliya specializes in maternal mental health, relationships, identity, immigrant experiences, and the emotional complexities of modern motherhood. She provides therapy in both Russian and English and is passionate about creating spaces where people feel seen, understood, and less alone. Her work is grounded not only in professional training, but also in lived experience — including the ongoing realities of motherhood, family life, immigration, and building a life and career in New York City.

In her free time, Yuliya enjoys running and has completed three 5K races in the last year. For her, running is a way to reconnect to her body and feel resilient and empowered. She also runs a book club for Gestalt therapists at Gestalt Associates for Psychotherapy in New York City and is passionate about building a professional circle of support for therapists.

About the Artist

Sharon Itkoff Nacache ATR-BC LCAT LPAT PMH-C is an artist, perinatal art therapist, educator, author, and proud mother of two spirited boys. She is thrilled to be collaborating with Yuliya as a fellow therapist mom and PMAD survivor herself, and is passionate about expanding the canopy of support for young families.

Sharon has over 16 years of clinical experience specializing in empowering those who identify as caregivers–personally or professionally–to cultivate creative resilience in the workplace, throughout their family-building journeys, and beyond. She is a trauma-informed, attachment-based, relational clinician with a virtual practice called Co-Create Art Therapy serving New Jersey and New York. Her expressive clinical approaches as a perinatal art therapist are grounded in principles of cultural humility, humanism, and the healing power of an empathic creative process.

Sharon is also a creative clinical consultant with the Whitney Museum of American Art, where she provides integrative arts-based wellness workshops for employees in both the public and private sectors to bring creative healing spaces to work and address caregiver burnout on the job. Her work has been featured in both the New York and LA Times, and her participatory perinatal picture book for expectant parents, called *The Days Before I Met You*, is available on Amazon.

www.ingramcontent.com/pod-product-compliance
Lightning Source LLC
LaVergne TN
LVHW022051200926
848481LV00003B/858
9798234165749